First World War
and Army of Occupation
War Diary
France, Belgium and Germany

29 DIVISION
86 Infantry Brigade
Royal Warwickshire Regiment
52 Battalion
1 May 1919 - 29 October 1919

WO95/2302/4

The Naval & Military Press Ltd
www.nmarchive.com
Published in association with The National Archives

Published by

The Naval & Military Press Ltd

Unit 10 Ridgewood Industrial Park,

Uckfield, East Sussex,

TN22 5QE England

Tel: +44 (0) 1825 749494

www.naval-military-press.com

www.nmarchive.com

This diary has been reprinted in facsimile from the original. Any imperfections are inevitably reproduced and the quality may fall short of modern type and cartographic standards.

© Crown Copyright
Images reproduced by permission of The National Archives, London, England, 2015.

Contents

Document type	Place/Title	Date From	Date To
Heading	WO95/2302/4		
Heading	Southern (Late 29th) Divn 86th Infy Bde 52nd Bn Roy Warwicks May-Oct 1919. To Indep Div Southern Bde.		
Heading	War Diary. Month Of May 1919. Of 52nd. Battn. Royal Warwickshire Regiment.		
War Diary	Mulheim	01/05/1919	12/05/1919
War Diary	Kurten	13/05/1919	27/05/1919
Heading	War Diary. Month Of June 1919 Of 52nd. Battn. Royal Warwickshire Regiment.		
War Diary	Kurten	01/06/1919	09/06/1919
War Diary	Gladbach	10/06/1919	18/06/1919
War Diary	Burscheid	19/06/1919	30/06/1919
War Diary	Kurten	01/06/1919	09/06/1919
War Diary	Gladbach	10/06/1919	18/06/1919
War Diary	Burscheid	19/06/1919	30/06/1919
Heading	War Diary. For Month Of July 1919. Of 52nd. Battn. Royal Warwickshire Regiment.		
War Diary	Burscheid	01/07/1919	01/07/1919
War Diary	Berg Gladbach	02/07/1919	16/07/1919
War Diary	Mulheim	17/07/1919	28/07/1919
Heading	War Diary. Month Of August 1919. 52nd. Battn. Royal Warwickshire Regiment.		
War Diary	Mulheim	01/08/1919	15/08/1919
War Diary	Kurten	01/09/1919	13/09/1919
War Diary	B. Gladbach	14/09/1919	29/10/1919

M995/2302/4

SOUTHERN (LATE 29TH) DIVN

86TH INFY BDE

52ND BN ROY WARWICKS
MAY – OCT 1919

To INDEP DIV
SOUTHERN Bde

Army Form W.3091.

Cover for Documents.

Nature of Enclosures.

WAR DIARY.

Month of May 1919.

of

52nd. Battn. Royal Warwickshire Regiment.

May - Dec
1919

Notes, or Letters written.

Army Form C. 2118.

WAR DIARY
or
INTELLIGENCE SUMMARY
(Erase heading not required.)

Place	Date	Hour	Summary of Events and Information	Remarks and references to Appendices
	May			
MULHEIM	1 to 4		Battalion in MULHEIM Guards and Posts	
			Lt.Col.PEARSON relinquishes duties of 2nd i/c and takes over command 1/5 Devons. Major JEVONS takes over duties of 2nd i/c	
	5 to 11		Battalion in MULHEIM, Guards and Posts	
	12		C. & D. Coys to BERG GLADBACH (relieved by 2 copies of 51st R.Warwicks Regt) billets in Paper Factory	
	13		Battalion relieves 53rd R.Warwicks in outpost area. A.Coy B.Coy & Hqrs to FORSTEN, BECHEN & KURTEN. C. & D. Coys from BERG GLADBACH TO JUNKERMUHLE & WIPPERFELD.	
KURTEN	14		Battalion in Outpost line	
	15 to 22		do Wiring of perimeter commenced	
	23		do B.Coy from BECHEN to BIESENBACH	
	24		do	
	27		do Major HART H.G. takes over 2nd i/c vice Major Jevons J.H.	
	30		do	
	31		do Wiring completed	

SKMorton
LIEUT. COL.
Cmdg 62nd Battalion
ROYAL WARWICKSHIRE REGIMENT.

Cover for Documents.

Nature of Enclosures.

WAR DIARY.

MONTH OF JUNE 1919

OF

52nd. Battn. ROYAL WARWICKSHIRE REGIMENT.

Notes, or Letters written.

Army Form C. 2118.

WAR DIARY for 1 to 30 June

INTELLIGENCE SUMMARY. 52 R. Warwicks Regt.

(Erase heading not required)

Instructions regarding War Diaries and Intelligence Summaries are contained in F. S. Regs., Part II. and the Staff Manual respectively. Title pages will be prepared in manuscript.

Place	Date	Hour	Summary of Events and Information	Remarks and references to Appendices
Kerken	June 1.	8 R. gk.	Battalion in Outpost Area.	BR
"	8.		Guards of 53 Royal Warwicks at GLADBACH relieved by the Battalion.	BR
GLADBACH	10.		Battalion moves to billets in paper factory GLADBACH relieving 53 R.W.R.	BR
"	17.		Instructions received that peace not being signed the advance into Germany would continue. Movement to begin on 20th.	BR
"	18.		All government stores sent to MULHEIM. All guards relieved by corps Heavy Artillery.	BR
Burscheid	19.		Battalion moved to BURSCHEID taking over billets from 53 Devons 25 Southern Brigade, arriving 16.30 hours. All moves for 20th cancelled.	BR
"	23.		Warning Order to move received.	BR
"	27.		Orders received later that Battalion will remain in BURSCHEID till further orders. Orders received for Battalion to move to BERG GLADBACH in the event of peace being signed.	BR
"	28.		Peace signed. Battalion ordered to move to BERG GLADBACH.	BR
"	30.		Guards at GLADBACH found by corps Heavy Artillery relieved on July 1st by the Battalion.	BR

S R Clayton ....LIEUT. COL.
Cmdg. 52nd BATTALION,
ROYAL WARWICKSHIRE REGIMENT.

52 Royal Warwickshire R/V
Army Form C. 2118.

WAR DIARY
or
INTELLIGENCE SUMMARY.
(Erase heading not required)

Instructions regarding War Diaries and Intelligence Summaries are contained in F. S. Regs., Part II. and the Staff Manual respectively. Title pages will be prepared in manuscript.

Place	Date	Hour	Summary of Events and Information	Remarks and references to Appendices
ST KURTEN	1		Bn in Outpost Area.	
	8th-9th		Guards of 53 rd. R. Warwicks at Gladbach relieved by Battalion.	
GLADBACH	10		Battalion moves to billets in Jopen Gaten Gladbach relieving 53rd. R. War. R.	
	14		Instructions received that troops not being required for the advance into Germany would continue movement to begin on 20th.	
"	18.		All Government Stores sent to Mulheim and all civilians and all Guards relieved by troops of Heavy Artillery.	
BORSCHEID	19.		Battalion moved to Burscheid, Kölner own billets from 53rd Devons. 2nd Borchin. leaving 1030 and arriving 1630 hrs. All movements for 20th cancelled.	
			Having orders to move received.	
	20		Orders received later that Battalion will remain in Burscheid till further orders.	
	24		Orders received for Battalion to move to Berg Gladbach in the event of these heavy dragoons leaving Battalion ordered to move to Gladbach on 1st July.	
	28			
	30		Guards at Gladbach found by troops of Heavy Artillery relieved by the Battalion.	

E R Clayton LIEUT. COL.
Cmdg. 52nd BATTALION,
ROYAL WARWICKSHIRE REGIMENT.

Cover for Documents.

Nature of Enclosures.

WAR DIARY.

FOR

MONTH OF JULY 1919.

OF

52nd. Battn. ROYAL WARWICKSHIRE REGIMENT.

Notes, or Letters written.

Army Form C. 2118.

52nd Battalion ~~WAR DIARY~~ Regiment.
INTELLIGENCE SUMMARY.

For the month of July 1919

(Erase heading not required.)

Instructions regarding War Diaries and Intelligence Summaries are contained in F. S. Regs, Part II. and the Staff Manual respectively. Title pages will be prepared in manuscript.

Place	Date	Hour	Summary of Events and Information	Remarks and references to Appendices
BURSCHEID	1		Battalion moved to BERG GLADBACH into Paper Factory billets vacated by II Corps Heavy Artillery	
BERG GLADBACH	2 - 15		Battalion at BERG GLADBACH	
	16		Guards of 53rd R.Warwicks at MULHEIM relieved by C.Coy	
			A. & B. Coys move to LEVERKUSEN & DELBRUCK.	
MULHEIM	17		Remainder of Battalion move to MULHEIM relieving 53rd R.Warwicks. Battalion Hqrs at 28 DUSSELDORFERSTRASSE.	
	18		A.Coy moves to FLITTARD from LEVERKUSEN.	
	22		B.Coy commences Rhine Army General Musketry Course at DELBRUCK.	
	26		B.Coy completes do	
	27		Inter Coy reliefs. A.Coy to MULHEIM relieving D.Coy D.Coy to DELBRUCK " B. " B.Coy to FLITTARD " A. "	
	28		D.Coy commences Rhine Army General Musketry Course.	

Army of the Rhine
1st August 1919.

S.R.Clay..........LIEUT. COL.
CMDG. 52ND BATTALION
ROYAL WARWICKSHIRE REGT.

Army Form W.3091.

Cover for Documents.

Nature of Enclosures.

WAR DIARY.

MONTH OF AUGUST 1919.

52nd. Battn. ROYAL WARWICKSHIRE REGIMENT.

Notes, or Letters written.

Army Form C. 2118.

WAR DIARY
or
INTELLIGENCE SUMMARY 52nd R.Warwicks Rgt

August

(Erase heading not required.)

Place	Date	Hour	Summary of Events and Information	Remarks and references to Appendices
MULHEIM.	1st		Battalion at MULHEIM	
	8th		Extra guard mounted on DOCKS. 2 N.C.O.s and 6 men.	
	14th		B.Coy at Flittard was relieved by Coy 51st R.Warwicks and moved to Paper Factory BERG GLADBACH. D.Coy at DELBRUCK relieved and moved to Paper Factory GLADBACH. Capt. H.Reid i/c of detachment at Paper Factory. All guards in MULHEIM relieved by 51st R.Warwicks.	
	15th		Battalion moved to KURTEN. Battalion Hqrs at KURTEN. Companies in outpost line being as follows :— A.Coy. JUNKERMUHLE. B.Coy. WIPPERFELD C.Coy. BECHEN (in reserve) D.Coy. FORSTEN.	

E.R.Clery LIEUT.COL.
CMDG 52ND BATTALION
ROYAL WARWICKSHIRE REGIMENT.

52ND BATTALION
ROYAL WARWICKSHIRE REGIMENT
1 SEP 1919
ORDERLY ROOM

Army Form C. 2118.

WAR DIARY
or
INTELLIGENCE SUMMARY.
(Erase heading not required.)

52 R.Warwicks

Instructions regarding War Diaries and Intelligence Summaries are contained in F. S. Regs., Part II. and the Staff Manual respectively. Title pages will be prepared in manuscript.

Place	Date	Hour	Summary of Events and Information	Remarks and references to Appendices
KURTEN.	1/9/19 to 12/9/19		Battalion on outpost duty in Forward Area.	
KURTEN.	12/9/19		Guards at BERG GLADBACH taken over from 53rd Royal Warwicks Regt.	
KURTEN.	13/9/19		Battalion relieved by 51st Royal Warwicks Regt. and moved to BERG GLADBACH in relief of 53rd Royal Warwicks Regt. "A" Coy detached to DELLBRUCK to fire General Musketry Course.	
B.GLADBACH	14/9/19 to 21/9/19		Billeted in BERG GLADBACH and "A" Coy under canvas at DELLBRUCK.	
B.GLADBACH	21/9/19		A.Coy. returns to BERG GLADBACH. "B" Coy proceed to DELLBRUCK to fire General Musketry Course.	
	22/9/19 to 30/9/19		Billeted in BERG GLADBACH. "C" Coy under Canvas at DELLBRUCK.	

S.R.Taufur
LIEUT. COL.
CMDG 52ND
ROYAL WARWICKSHIRE REGIMENT

WAR DIARY
INTELLIGENCE SUMMARY
(Erase heading not required.)

Army Form C. 2118.

5.2 R. Warwicks

Place	Date	Hour	Summary of Events and Information	Remarks and references to Appendices
B.GLADBACH.	Oct. 1.		Battalion billeted in Paper Factory. C.Coy. at DELLBRUCK. firing General Musketry Course.	W
	2		C.Coy. returned from DELLBRUCK to BERG GLADBACH.	W
	3		Major I.H.MACDONELL D.S.O. Highland Light Infantry, assumed duties of 2nd in Command vice Major W.J.T.CARDER 5th Devon. Regt.	W
	21		Major MACDONELL proceeded to MULHEIM to command detachment 52nd R.Warwick Rgt. composed of 53rd Bttn. to be transferred to 51st and 52nd on disbandment of 53rd.	W
	23		Major MACDONELL i/c troops MULHEIM sub area.	W
	24		C. & D.Coy. (325 N.C.O.s and men) of 53rd R.W.R. transferred to 52nd R.W.Rgt. and taken on strength with effect from and including 24th inst. Capt. W.N.SETTLE Lancs. Fusiliers. Capt. J.G.D.DUNBAR. Gloucester Rgt. 2/Lieut. SHARP A.B. R.Warwicks Rgt. } posted to Battalion. 2/Lieut HUTCHINGS W. R.Warwicks Rgt. } " HERITAGE H.R. 2/4 Hants Rgt. }	W
	25		A. & C.Coys move from GLADBACH to MULHEIM absorbing transfers from 53rd R.W.Rgt.	W
	27		Capt. SETTLE took over pay and command of D.Coy. from Capt. H.C.W.REID. 2/Lt. J.B.WITHERICK 7th Warwicks. posted to Battalion. Lieut H.A.de F.FORD R.Warwicks. " "	W
	29.		A. & C.Coys returned to GLADBACH from MULHEIM. D.Coy. moved to DELLBRUCK to take over duties at Prisoner of War Camp.	W

www.ingramcontent.com/pod-product-compliance
Lightning Source LLC
Chambersburg PA
CBHW081254170426
43191CB00037B/2150